TopGear

100

FASTEST CARS

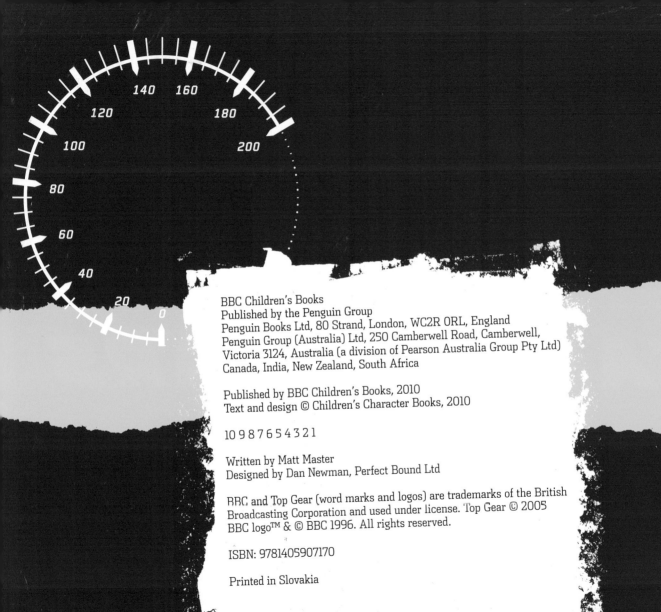

BBC Children's Books
Published by the Penguin Group
Penguin Books Ltd, 80 Strand, London, WC2R 0RL, England
Penguin Group (Australia) Ltd, 250 Camberwell Road, Camberwell,
Victoria 3124, Australia (a division of Pearson Australia Group Pty Ltd)
Canada, India, New Zealand, South Africa

Published by BBC Children's Books, 2010
Text and design © Children's Character Books, 2010

10 9 8 7 6 5 4 3 2 1

Written by Matt Master
Designed by Dan Newman, Perfect Bound Ltd

ISBN: 9781405907170

Printed in Slovakia

Contents

Introduction

In the name of research, *Top Gear* has spent thousands of hours going fast on the *Top Gear* Test Track. After countless years, miles and miles per gallon, this is the ultimate list: *Top Gear's* 100 Fastest Cars.

Some of them you'll know very well, some you may never have heard of. Some are brand new, some so old even your dad won't remember them. But trust us, this is the list to end all lists.

It's not about 0-60mph. And it's not about top speed. It's not even about how fast the Stig can get round our track. It's more about that thing you can't really explain; that makes your eyes narrow and your hands shake. These are the hundred coolest cars that ever went fast. These things are the reason that *Top Gear* gets up in the morning, and the reason it can't get to sleep at night...

 Cool Rating 😀😀😀😀😀

It goes without saying that no car in this book is entirely uncool (by which we mean a bit warm and clammy), but this **Stigometer** should help separate the merely chilly, with one helmet, from the seriously Subzero – with five.

Aston Martin
DBS

If there is one person in the world that every car maker wants the official seal of approval from, it's got to be James Bond. Happily for Aston Martin he seems to like the DBS these days, just so long as it's fitted with a few hidden extras.

Aston's 510bhp V12 super coupé is the ultimate blend of luxury and sporting ability, being both stupendously fast and posher inside than a private jet.

Although no match for its rivals from Ferrari and Lamborghini for pure pace, it exists in an entirely cooler world full of glamorous parties, beautiful girls and deadly secret agents. OK, maybe not the secret agents, but you get the idea.

Power: 510bhp

0-60mph: 4.3 seconds

Top Speed: 191mph

Price: £170,500

Cool rating:

TT=378-20

01

02

AC Cobra
1964

In the sixties a tiny British sports car company called AC was busy making a pretty little two-seater called the Ace. It was the sort of thing you took your girlfriend out in, maybe for a picnic in the countryside.

Meanwhile, in the USA, a burly chap in a cowboy hat called Caroll Shelby was tuning up enormous V8 engines and wondering what to do with them. You can guess what happened next.

The AC Cobra rocked the racing world and went on to become one of the most iconic road cars of all time. Simple, beautiful and with a turn of speed more commonly seen in surface-to-air missiles, there are few cars that capture the vision of a sports car more perfectly.

Power: *260bhp*

0-60mph: *5.5 seconds*

Top Speed: *138mph*

Price: *£2500 (1967)*

Cool rating:

Vauxhall VXR8
Bathurst

DE51 RED

'I just **love** the sound of a supercharger!'

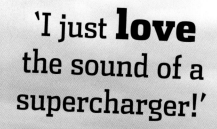

I gnore the Vauxhall badge. This is really a Holden, the Australian alternative to Vauxhall. What that means is that instead of a boring man with a briefcase and sandals, you get a hairy bloke in a sweaty vest.

The VXR8 is a car so macho that it makes rugby players hide behind their mums' skirts. It has a huge supercharged V8 taken straight out of the latest Corvette and creates enough noise when you stamp on the fast pedal to make animals drop dead in sub-Saharan Africa. When you're in Leeds. It's not very good to drive, but that's hardly the point is it?

 Power: *564bhp*

 0-60mph: *4.6 seconds*

 Top Speed: *155mph*

 Price: *£45,000*

 Cool rating:

Even very sensible people like the men who work at Volkswagen have days when things go a bit loopy. Bored of putting 105bhp 1.6-litre engines into Golfs, a few mechanics decided to pinch a 6.0-litre 12-cylinder engine from the Phaeton limousine, bolt on two turbochargers and then see if they could squeeze it into a GTI.

Needless to say it didn't fit under the bonnet so they put it where the back seats were meant to be.

VW says that the 641bhp Golf W12 is capable of hitting 202mph. But it also says there are no plans to make more and sell them to the likes of us. (See. Back to being sensible again.)

 Power: 641bhp

 0-60mph: 3.7 seconds

 Top Speed: 202mph

 Price: Not for sale

 Cool rating:

'It is an **insane** car, this.'

04

VW Golf W12

 05

Not everyone realises that Lamborghini started out making tractors. But anyone who ever bought a Countach worked it out pretty fast. Despite looking like it could go to the moon and back before most normal cars had even started, Lamborghini's eighties icon was a bit of a pig to drive.

It was enormous for a start, which never helps, and you needed legs like Mr Universe to operate the pedals. You couldn't see out of the back at all either, which made reverse parking an act of blind faith. Often a very expensive act at that.

But point a Countach down a windy mountain road and all was forgiven. This was a car that was made for that one thing, and

is hopeless at everything else.

 Power: *375bhp*

 0-60mph: *6.8 seconds*

 Top Speed: *196 mph*

 Price: *£17,000 (1974)*

 Cool rating: 😎😎😎😎

05 Lamborghini
Countach

06

Gumpert

Apollo

D IN
AP 2000

18

'Ye gods! This is just something else.'

By the skin of its (probably very sharp) teeth, the Gumpert is the fastest car round the *Top Gear* track. Less than a second separates the top five, but this ugly-as-sin supercar has it by a whisker.

Really just a racing car with boring bits like lights and indicators stuck on afterwards, the Apollo can hit 225mph, but will cost you £275,000 for the privilege.

Gumpert claims that, thanks to clever aerodynamics and general scary speediness, you could drive the Apollo upside down on the roof of a tunnel. Surprisingly they haven't found anyone willing to give it a go yet though.

 Power: 789bhp

 0-60mph: 3.2 seconds

 Top Speed: 225mph

 Price: £275,000

 Cool rating:

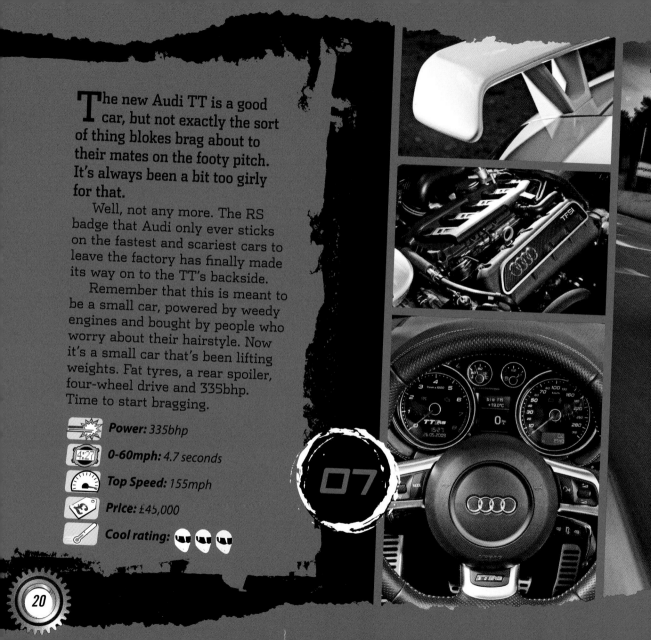

The new Audi TT is a good car, but not exactly the sort of thing blokes brag about to their mates on the footy pitch. It's always been a bit too girly for that.

Well, not any more. The RS badge that Audi only ever sticks on the fastest and scariest cars to leave the factory has finally made its way on to the TT's backside.

Remember that this is meant to be a small car, powered by weedy engines and bought by people who worry about their hairstyle. Now it's a small car that's been lifting weights. Fat tyres, a rear spoiler, four-wheel drive and 335bhp. Time to start bragging.

Power: 335bhp

0-60mph: 4.7 seconds

Top Speed: 155mph

Price: £45,000

Cool rating: 🏁🏁🏁

07

07

Audi TT

RS

Renault Clio
Williams

In the nineties, Williams was the team to beat in Formula 1 and the engines it used were made by Renault. This sort of partnership is very good for business, so the bosses at Renault decided to sign off a sporty version of the first Clio with Williams badges all over it.

The truth was that Williams had absolutely nothing to do with the car, but that didn't matter a jot to Renault. Or the people that bought them, as it turned out. Sticking a powerful two-litre engine into a tiny French hatchback and making it wider, lower and meaner-looking, created a car that people still beg, borrow and steal to get hold of today.

 Power: 145bhp

 0-60mph: 7.8 seconds

 Top Speed: 134mph

 Price: £13,000

 Cool rating: 👓👓

08

Ford Escort Cosworth

09

K38

When the Escort Cosworth went on sale in the early nineties it was an instant hit with a certain type of British bloke. And that type included one Jeremy Clarkson. Here was a bit of honest, local metal that looked like a cross between a proper racing car and a bouncer.

It had four-wheel drive, a huge twin-fin rear wing and a turbocharged Cosworth engine that people could, and regularly did, tune up to dizzying levels of power.

The only real drawback was that everybody wanted one and it was easy to steal. So that tended to happen rather a lot.

 Power: 224bhp

 0-60mph: 6.3 seconds

 Top Speed: 138mph

 Price: £26,000

 Cool rating: 👽👽👽

Lotus rewrote the rules when it launched the first Elise way back in 1996. Here was a car that offered its driver almost nothing that you'd expect from normal 20th century transport. It was cramped, uncomfortable, had pretty much zero storage space, no back seats and even the stereo was an optional extra.

But it was more fun than a lifetime ticket to Alton Towers, and occasionally just as likely to make you feel sick.

So if you were willing to put up with a little discomfort, for the same money as a boring old hatchback, you could buy one of the best-handling cars of all time. And a lot of people did.

 Power: 118bhp

 0-60mph: 5.5 seconds

Top Speed: 124mph

Price: £19,000

Cool rating: 👽👽👽

10

10

Lotus Elise
S1

Ferrari 250
GTO

It may be one of the oldest cars in this book, but the Ferrari 250 GTO is also one of the greatest. Built to go racing in the early sixties, the GTO was an instant success on the track and just as quickly became immensely desirable in road-going trim.

With its blend of staggering performance for the time and the sort of looks that made men faint just as quickly as their girlfriends, it soon became one of the most sought-after Ferraris of all time.

So much so, in fact, that in 2008 a GTO is rumoured to have sold for £15.7 million. You could probably buy the moon for that.

 Power: 300bhp

 0-60mph: 6.1 seconds

 Top Speed: 173mph

 Price: £6000 (1962)

 Cool rating: 🏁🏁🏁🏁🏁

11

29

Mercedes CLK
GTR

12

The best way to make people think your cars are good is to win races in them. And if this isn't possible, maybe because your cars are a bit rubbish, then the next best thing is to make an unbelievably high-tech, lightweight race-rocket, and dress it up as one of your cars.

Mercedes aren't the only ones to have done this, but what they claimed was a CLK coupé under all the carbon fibre, wings and spoilers of their 215mph V12 racer was probably the furthest ever from road-going reality.

When it went on sale the GTR was also the most expensive production car in the world, costing over £1 million. And had a tendency to set itself on fire. These two facts don't sit all that well together, do they?

Power: 720bhp

0-60mph: 3.4 seconds

Top Speed: 215mph

Price: £1.1 million (1998)

Cool rating: ●●●●

Porsche 911
GT1

There used to be a strange rule in sports car racing that said you had to sell a certain number of street-legal versions of whichever model you wanted to race. This was annoying for car companies but brilliant for us, because it meant Porsche had to make things like the GT1.

Although designed specifically to win the Le Mans 24 Hours, 25 GT1s were turned into road cars and sold to a lucky (and very wealthy) few.

Loosely based on the 911 of the time, the GT1 managed to squeeze around 700bhp from that car's 3.2-litre 6-cylinder engine and is rumoured to have been able to reach 235mph. Corking.

Power: 700bhp

0-60mph: 3.3 seconds

Top Speed: 235mph

Price: £550,000

Cool rating:

14

Plymouth Roadrunner
Superbird

Looking more like something from a cartoon than a car factory, the Plymouth Superbird was the stuff of every American schoolboy's dreams back in 1970. It was a muscle car in the purest sense of the word, with a massive V8 up front sending huge dollops of power to the rear via a four-speed stick (that's a manual gearbox to us Brits).

The Superbird was one of those ultra-rare cars that got built to allow Plymouth to race in NASCAR, the fastest and most popular American motorsport. So that three-foot high rear wing wasn't for show, but had to keep the Superbird glued to the tarmac at racing speeds. Utterly terrifying.

 Power: *425bhp*

 0-60mph: *4.8 seconds*

 Top Speed: *200mph*

 Price: *US$4,000 (1970)*

 Cool rating: 🌡🌡🌡🌡

The original Lotus Esprit is one of the greatest shapes in the whole history of cars. It looked more like a paper dart than something with wheels and an engine, and weighed about as much as one too.

Everyone remembers the white one that James Bond drove underwater, but the normal car you could actually buy was just as good. Well, nearly.

It didn't have a big engine, or much power, and it went wrong an awful lot, but the great thing about the Lotus Esprit was how it handled. This made it fast in the corners and that made it fun. It was also made mostly of plastic which meant that, unlike most cars from the seventies, it didn't start rusting the day you bought it.

 Power: *160bhp*

 0-60mph: *6.8 seconds*

 Top Speed: *138mph*

 Price: *£7883 (1976)*

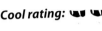 **Cool rating:**

Lotus Esprit
S1

15

15

Minis are an OK sort of car, but they do tend to be bought by mums and people that worry about their hair. And they're not very fast. Which is why God ordered someone to build the John Cooper Works.

This is a Mini with a hairy chest and a big gold medallion round its neck. And it's very fast indeed. (It might not have been God's idea though. We just made that bit up).

The JCW matches some seriously beefy bodywork with a supercharged engine. The result is a Mini that makes you need to pop to the loo, partly out of fear and partly out of sheer excitement.

Well done, Mini. Well done, God.

Power: 208bhp

0-60mph: 6.5 seconds

Top Speed: 143mph

Price: £21,000

Cool rating:

16

MINI Cooper JCW

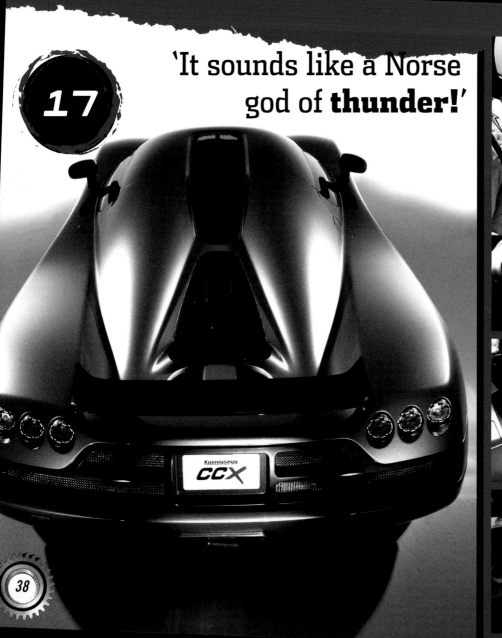

17

'It sounds like a Norse god of **thunder!**'

Sweden is a sensible country. Everything is very clean and tidy. Everyone is very polite. And Sweden makes Volvos, which are the world's most sensible cars. (And probably the dullest. Shhh.)

But tucked away in a quiet corner of the Swedish countryside is a place that makes the Koenigsegg CCX, the only car that has ever made the Stig need to call his mum.

This 806bhp monster is capable of reaching 245mph, making it one of the fastest road cars on planet Earth. And one of the scariest. After the Stig crashed one in 2008, *Top Gear* had to put a spoiler on it. Just to make his mum leave us alone.

 Power: 806bhp

 0-60mph: 3.2 seconds

 Top Speed: 245mph

Price: £405,000

Cool rating:

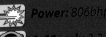

Koenigsegg CCX

(with the *Top Gear* spoiler)

Chevrolet
Camaro

Like its arch rival the Ford Mustang, the new Camaro is the reincarnation of a classic sixties muscle car. This means that it looks sort of old, sort of new, and like it's spent the last year locked in a gym.

Slotting the same V8 that powers the Corvette beneath its beefy body, the Camaro is that typical American mix of simplicity and power, with 426bhp fed to the rear wheels via a traditional manual gearbox.

In the USA a Camaro is cheap too, which makes you forget how rubbishy and plastic it feels, but evil things like tax make it very expensive in the UK. Expensive and still rubbishy and plastic? That's not so good.

 Power: 426bhp

 0-60mph: 4.7 seconds

 Top Speed: 155mph

 Price: £21,000

 Cool rating: 🚗🚗🚗

Although people are calling it 'The Baby Rolls', the Ghost is still more expensive than most peoples' houses, and about the same size.

Based on the not-very-babyish BMW 7-Series, and housing a not-even-remotely babyish 6.6-litre V12 under its enormous bonnet, the Ghost is still posh enough for the Prime Minister (probably far too posh actually), but as fast as most sports cars half its size.

It's almost 18 feet long and weighs more than Wales, but it can get to 60mph in well under five seconds and has been limited to 155mph. Just in case.

 Power: 563bhp

 0-60mph: 4.7 seconds

 Top Speed: 155mph

 Price: £195,000

 Cool rating: 😎😎

19

Rolls-Royce
GHOST

19

43

However big the engine, however sleek the bodywork, it's almost impossible to design a supercar that can outpace an Evo.

Using a really basic four-door saloon, but then sticking in all sorts of ingenious technology developed for racing rally cars, Mitsubishi can turn a shopping cart into a go-kart, producing something capable of giving a £200,000 Lamborghini Murcielago a run for its money. And for a quarter of the price.

The FQ400 gets 403bhp from a 2.0-litre, 4-cylinder engine while the Lambo has 631bhp from an engine three times the size. Makes you want to pay more attention in science class. Almost.

 Power: 403bhp

 0-60mph: 3.8 seconds

 Top Speed: 155mph

 Price: £50,000

 Cool rating:

Mitsubishi Evo X
FQ400

20

'It is genuinely **incredible.** There is no car that handles like this one.'

While most really fast cars these days have their engines behind the driver and tend to look like ballistic missiles with wheels, Mercedes is doing it all very differently.

The SLS is a seriously modern supercar, but they've styled it on one of their most elegant sports cars from the sixties, the 300SL Gullwing.

This means the engine is out in front under a long, menacing bonnet, and best of all, it also means you get those unbelievably cool gullwing doors. Definitely the car to have if you need to get places in a hurry but want to turn up looking sub-zero.

 Power: 563bhp

 0-60mph: 3.8 seconds

 Top Speed: 197mph

 Price: £130,000

 Cool rating:

21

Mercedes SLS

21

'It looks good, it **sounds good** and it even puts a smile on your face every time the back end sets off on its own.'

MG SV

In the olden days MG was a brand for men with beards. And it still is come to think of it. But a few years ago, just before the company disappeared for good, it was about to launch a radical new sports car that would have blown the polyester socks off the old MG brigade.

The SV was a serious proposition, made entirely of carbon fibre to save weight and powered by a ferocious American V8 that could be tuned to up to 1,000bhp.

Or at least that's what MG said. Unfortunately we never got to find out because the money ran out before they could finish building the thing.

 Power: *320bhp*

 0-60mph: *5.3 seconds*

 Top Speed: *165mph*

 Price: *£75,000*

 Cool rating:

Honda NSX
Type R

23

A few years ago it was accepted everywhere in the world that Honda only made cars for Grandma. The only people that weren't happy about this were Honda. So they decided to build the NSX, a supercar to thrash Ferrari.

There was a lot of chuckling and raising of eyebrows, and then the NSX actually turned up. And it was amazing. It looked the business, went like stink and, best of all, was still as reliable and easy to use as Grandma's Honda Civic.

The last few ever made got the Type R treatment, which meant they were lighter, had racing suspension and were only ever painted white. A *Top Gear* hero.

 Power: *276bhp*

 0-60mph: *4.4 seconds*

 Top Speed: *168mph*

 Price: *£70,000 (–ish)*

 Cool rating: 🌡🌡🌡🌡🌡

23

Porsche Cayenne
GTS

54

24

The Cayenne is one of those terrible cars favoured by footballers' wives and people with huge sunglasses and fake tans. Oh, that's footballers' wives again. Anyway, it's pretty awful. Not a proper Porsche, more of a posh handbag with four-wheel drive.

But the GTS is a bit different. Only a bit, mind, because it's still a terrible show-off, but at least this one drives like a Porsche should. It's quick, has a superb manual gearbox and handles better than any other SUV on sale today.

If you simply *have* to have a Cayenne (and you really don't, y'know?) then this is the only acceptable choice.

Power: *399bhp*

0-60mph: *6.1 seconds*

Top Speed: *157mph*

Price: *£54,500*

Cool rating:

Ferrari
458 Italia

FE 458 ITA

25

Every time Ferrari launches a new car the world is left dumbstruck. Can it really look like that? Can it really go that fast? And the answer is always 'Yes'.

The 458 is Ferrari's latest mid-engine sports car, the model that will have every premiership footballer on the phone to his local dealer, begging and pleading and generally making a fool of himself.

It's worth the embarrassment though. The 458 is that perfect blend of stunning looks and astonishing performance. The V8 engine behind the driver pumps out 562bhp via a flappy paddle gearbox that borrows technology from Ferrari's latest Formula 1 car.

And one of the brains behind the 458 is none other than Michael Schumacher, just in case you were still having any doubts.

 Power: *562bhp*

 0-60mph: *3.4 seconds*

 Top Speed: *202mph*

 Price: *£160,000*

 Cool rating:

'The acceleration is so **brutal!**'

26

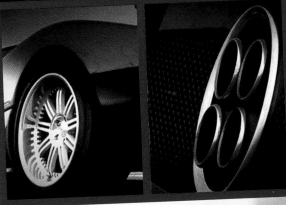

Pagani Zonda F
Roadster

26

This is the car that even our very own Captain Slow fell in love with. Probably because the Zonda is everything a supercar needs to be: stunningly beautiful, absolutely unaffordable and insanely (by which we mean put it in a padded cell) fast.

With a 7.3-litre V12 engine borrowed from Mercedes, squeezed into a car that weighs as much as not very many tins of baked beans, the Zonda F Roadster will go from 0-120mph in less than 10 seconds, and then get back to nought again in half that. It will, however, cost you £825,000 to try this, or it would if you could still buy a Zonda F. Which you can't. Sorry.

 Power: 641bhp

 0-60mph: 3.6 seconds

 Top Speed: 214mph

 Price: £825,000

 Cool rating: 🙂🙂🙂🙂🙂

This is one of those cars that comes about because someone got really bored at work and their boss was off sick. When else does it seem like a good idea to stick a 3.0-litre V6 engine in the back of a Renault Clio?

The Renaultsport Clio V6 looks meaner than a pitbull in a biker jacket, but that's pretty much where the good news ends. Yes, it's very fast in a straight line, but keeping it in a straight line is almost impossible. There's also no room in there because the engine's in the wrong place. And to make matters worse, Renault had to make the V6 stupendously expensive to buy and *still* lost money on every one they ever made.

 Power: 255bhp

 0-60mph: 5.8 seconds

 Top Speed: 153mph

 Price: £27,000

 Cool rating: 😎😎

27

Renaultsport
Clio V6

5945 WWT 92

Audi Sport Quattro

Nowadays it's quite normal for an ordinary-looking car to have four-wheel drive, but thirty years ago this was a technology reserved for smelly farm vehicles and soldiers. Then the Audi Sport Quattro came along, a car that turned rally driving on its head by giving its drivers twice the grip of anyone else in the race.

This advantage quickly found its way into Audi's road cars, and suddenly four-wheel drive was everywhere, eventually cropping up in Porsches and Lamborghinis.

The Sport Quattro was the ultimate road-going version of Audi's rally-winning coupé, with a shortened, lighter body made from the same material as bulletproof vests, which is a brilliant idea whichever way you look at it.

 Power: 302bhp

 0-60mph: 4.8 seconds

 Top Speed: 155mph

 Price: £50,000 (1984)

 Cool rating: 👽👽👽👽👽

When Jaguar announced it was going to make the greatest car in the world, a lot of people swallowed the bait, paying huge sums of money up front to ensure that they got one first. After all, the XJ220 was going to be Britain's first mid-engine, V12, 200mph, four-wheel drive supercar. This they had to have.

Sadly, when it finally turned up it had an engine half the size and rear-wheel drive. And no ABS brakes. Oh, and the final price had gone up by £40,000.

The XJ220 still did well over 200mph, but everyone was a bit gloomy about it by then and they all wanted the Ferrari F40 instead.

Power: 542bhp

0-60mph: 3.6 seconds

Top Speed: 213mph

Price: £403,000

Cool rating:

29

Jaguar
XJ220

29

30

There was a time when Aston Martin only made cars for really posh old men instead of footballers and people who've won the lottery. And back then the big, boxy V8 Vantage was Aston's sportiest model.

It had similar technology to a steam train and was even worse at going round corners.

But it was a lot better at going in a straight line.

This is what fans of ancient and rather rubbishy British engineering call 'point and squirt', meaning you point your car up the road, stamp on the gas and hope there isn't much call for turning the wheel.

It's a lot of fun and more than a little bit scary.

 Power: *438bhp*

 0-60mph: *5.4 seconds*

 Top Speed: *168mph*

 Price: *£20,000 (1977)*

 Cool rating:

Aston Martin
V8 Vantage (Original)

 30

31

BMW don't muck about when it comes to building a fast car. But there is a company that still thinks they have a thing or two to learn.

Alpina is a little German outfit that has been giving BMWs a boost for over fifty years, so they definitely know their stuff. Sadly, when they got hold of the Z8, they turned it into the sort of car your granddad would use to find nice picnic spots.

Jeremy described driving the normal Z8 round a corner as 'like trying to get a wardrobe up a fire escape', and Alpina made it even more soggy and hopeless. Fast, and very beautiful, but a terrible way to spend £95,000.

 Power: 375bhp

 0-60mph: 5.0 seconds

 Top Speed: 161mph

 Price: £95,000

 Cool rating:

BMW Z8
Alpina

31

Roush Mustang

When Ford brought out the new Mustang we all got quite excited. Until we found out it was rubbish. Another cheap, badly made American car that didn't go round corners and couldn't even go very fast in a straight line.

Then along came Roush. This team of slightly bonkers racing experts fitted a supercharger to the Mustang, taking the power up to a whopping 450bhp. And that was the easy bit. Then they set about making the Mustang handle properly – and did a pretty amazing job of that too.

But the most impressive thing about the Roush Mustang is that it's still as cheap as a half-decent Volkswagen. If only we all lived in Texas.

Power: 450bhp

0-60mph: 4.3 seconds

Top Speed: 164mph

Price: £34,000

Cool rating:

32

This is the car that car nerds like us lot at *Top Gear* almost always call 'the most beautiful car in the history of the world ever'. Or something like that. The Miura really put Lamborghini on the map back in the 1960s and even now it is one of the most sought-after supercars for mega-rich collectors and film stars.

Truth be told, it was never actually very good. The designers put the fuel tank in the front and the engine in the middle, so that as you used up the petrol, the Miura began to do an involuntary wheelie. Not ideal at speeds of over 150mph. But no one cared then and no one cares now. Just look at it!

 Power: *350bhp*

 0-60mph: *6.2 seconds*

 Top Speed: *172mph*

 Price: *£6500 (1966)*

 Cool rating: 👽👽👽👽👽

33

Lamborghini
Miura

This is one of those cars that, like Marmite, you either love or hate. The Alfa Romeo SZ can make girls swoon, but at the same time it'll probably make a few babies cry. In fact it was nicknamed *Il Mostro*, which is Italian for The Monster, and that was by the people who liked it.

But the SZ wasn't just about those weird looks. Brilliant engineering and the adventurous use of lightweight plastics meant that it was actually a fantastic car to drive.

Alfa made so few SZs that they are a very rare sight these days. But maybe you think that's a good thing...

 Power: 210bhp

0-60mph: 6.9 seconds

Top Speed: 153mph

Price: £40,000 (1989)

Cool rating:

34

34

Alfa Romeo
sz

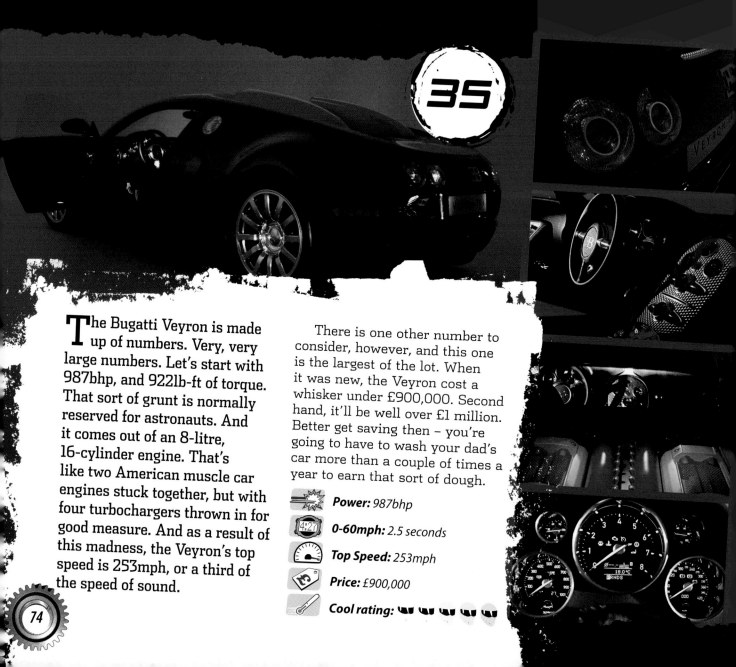

The Bugatti Veyron is made up of numbers. Very, very large numbers. Let's start with 987bhp, and 922lb-ft of torque. That sort of grunt is normally reserved for astronauts. And it comes out of an 8-litre, 16-cylinder engine. That's like two American muscle car engines stuck together, but with four turbochargers thrown in for good measure. And as a result of this madness, the Veyron's top speed is 253mph, or a third of the speed of sound.

There is one other number to consider, however, and this one is the largest of the lot. When it was new, the Veyron cost a whisker under £900,000. Second hand, it'll be well over £1 million. Better get saving then – you're going to have to wash your dad's car more than a couple of times a year to earn that sort of dough.

Power: *987bhp*

0-60mph: *2.5 seconds*

Top Speed: *253mph*

Price: *£900,000*

Cool rating:

35

Bugatti
Veyron

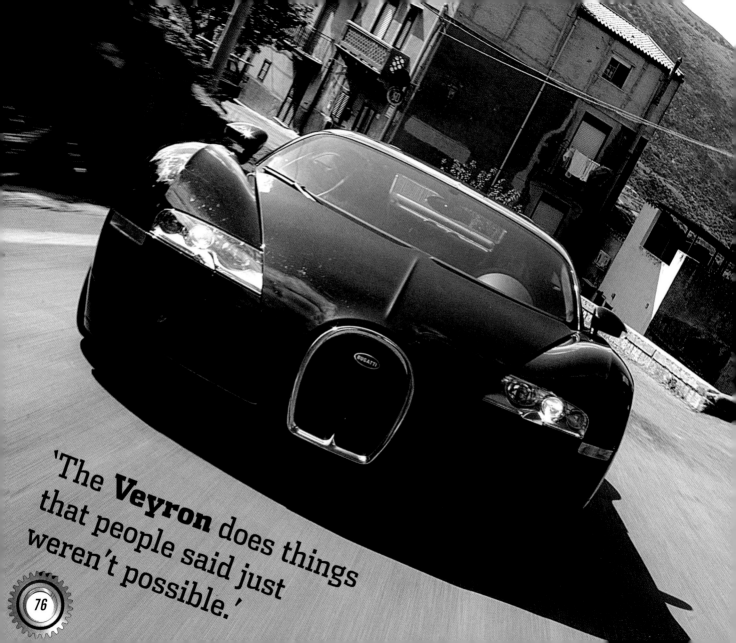

'The **Veyron** does things that people said just weren't possible.'

'That is proper head-alteringly **quick.**'

Noble M600

M600 GB

36

We Brits have a long and slightly iffy history of building plastic sports cars in leaky barns that are meant to be better than the latest Ferrari. Very occasionally they are, but mostly they don't even start.

Noble has made a fair few cars that are more familiar to the AA than their owners, but hopefully the brand new M600 will change all that.

With a twin-turbo V8 generating 650bhp nestled into a lightweight carbon fibre body, it's going to be faster than almost anything else on the road. And at £200,000 there won't be much that's more expensive. Fingers crossed it works...

 Power: 650bhp

 0-60mph: 3.0 seconds

 Top Speed: 225mph

 Price: £200,000

 Cool rating:

37

SMG 656

The logic behind the Viper is very simple. Big things have big engines. So why not take the 8.4-litre 10-cylinder engine and gearbox from an enormous truck and stick it in a sports car?

Turns out there are a lot of reasons why not. Driving the SRT-10 is still like driving a truck, just an unbelievably fast one that appears to have been made out of recycled crisp packets.

The Viper looks tremendous and sounds like a mad thing, but it's terrible at going round corners. In other words it's utterly useless unless you fancy towing the world's fastest caravan.

Power: 500bhp

0-60mph: 3.8 seconds

Top Speed: 190mph

Price: £70,000

Cool rating:

Dodge Viper
SRT-10

Bentley
Flying Spur

Going fast isn't just a young man's game. Even slightly podgy old men with no hair like to go fast, but preferably if someone else is doing the driving. Which must be why the Bentley Flying Spur exists.

This gigantic 600bhp 6.0-litre 12-cylinder limousine weighs almost 2.5 tonnes and is more spacious and luxurious inside than most five-star hotel rooms. But it can still hit 200mph and find 60mph in 4.5 seconds. Which is utterly bonkers when you think about it.

It's not great at going round corners though, so it's probably best to simply clamber into the back, put your slippers on, your feet up and let Jeeves do all the hard work.

 Power: 600bhp

 0-60mph: 4.5 seconds

 Top Speed: 200mph

 Price: £140,000

 Cool rating:

38

83

Subaru made its name winning every rally going and then bunging all the technology from that into its road cars. Because of this, the Impreza is regarded as the only choice if you have to tackle a lot of winding country roads and are in an awful hurry. (Maybe if you're a burglar who's just robbed a chicken farm.)

Lots of whooshy turbo power, bags of four-wheel drive grip, ridiculous-looking wings, spoilers everywhere and incredibly ugly styling all add up to one of the greatest yet most embarrassing cars in this book.

We love it, but wouldn't want anyone to see us driving it.

 Power: 296bhp

 0-60mph: 4.8 seconds

 Top Speed: 155mph

 Price: £26,000

 Cool rating:

BN02 GRK

39

Subaru Impreza
WRX STi

If you're going to name a car after the man that started the company, it had better be seriously good. And the boffins at Ferrari made sure the Enzo was the best.

Back in 2003 when it went on sale, the Enzo was ridiculously high-tech, with a skeleton chassis made entirely of carbon fibre and a 6.0-litre V12 that borrowed ideas from Ferrari's championship-winning Formula 1 cars.

There is a drawback to making cars this fast though. Only 400 Enzos ever left the Ferrari factory, and after a series of very high-profile accidents, there are a fair few less than that still on the road today.

'For sheer excitement it's hard to think of **anything** that can match it.'

40

 Power: 650bhp

 0-60mph: 3.14 seconds

 Top Speed: 218mph

 Price: £450,000

 Cool rating:

Ferrari

Enzo

ferrari

MO·140·EF

A few years ago, Porsche started building a brand new racing car, but for reasons known only to German men in grey suits, they suddenly decided to stop. But having spent rather a lot of money on it already, someone insisted they turn the thing into a road car.

And so the Carrera GT was born, a thing so utterly terrifying that it is only mentioned in a hushed whisper in dark corners of the *Top Gear* office. Here was a car with all the performance of the world's greatest supercars, but without the high-tech driver aids that drivers of the world's greatest supercars tend to rely on rather a lot. Porsche never made many Carrera GTs, and most of them ended up in ditches.

 Power: 612bhp

 0-60mph: 3.9 seconds

 Top Speed: 205mph

 Price: £330,000

 Cool rating:

41

'The most **exciting** road-going car Porsche has ever made.'

Porsche Carrera GT

41

S GO 612

42

Peugeot 205
GTi

France has always had a reputation for making slightly rubbish cars that are surprisingly good fun to drive. Perhaps the best example of this is the Peugeot 205 GTi.

On the face of it, here's a very ordinary little hatchback, the sort of thing a librarian might buy, preferably in brown. But stick a high-revving injection engine under the bonnet and suddenly you have a shopping trolley for Formula 1 drivers.

The 205 GTi is one of the original and best hot hatches, although it's always had a bit of a reputation for going through hedges instead of round corners.

So, a *Top Gear* favourite, but one that needs to be treated with serious caution.

 Power: *105bhp*

 0-60mph: *8.6 seconds*

 Top Speed: *120mph*

 Price: *£6295 (1984)*

 Cool rating: 🏎️🏎️🏎️

90

Don't ask why BMW named its only real supercar after a British motorway. They must have had their reasons. What's important is that they made this thing at all.

The M1 was a racing project from the late seventies that never really took off, mostly because BMW teamed up with Lamborghini to build the thing and back then Lambo couldn't organise a barbecue in a butcher's shop.

So the M1 just ended up being an incredibly rare and capable road car, and the only BMW ever built with its engine behind the driver. In its day it was seriously quick, and even now the experts are still surprised by just how good the M1 is to drive.

 Power: *277bhp*

 0-60mph: *6.5 seconds*

 Top Speed: *163mph*

 Price: *£37,500 (1978)*

 Cool rating:

BMW

M1

43

Where the BMW M3 and Audi RS4 have to make do with measly 4 and 4.2-litre V8s to get around, the Mercedes C63 AMG gets one with 6.2 litres. That's a lot more, and more, as we all know, is better.

This means it has more power than its rivals of course, but more importantly, much more torque. Torque is weird and we don't really understand it, but it's what you'd use to pull a tree out of the ground. Or to accelerate like a nuclear missile when you needed to overtake something slow and annoying.

The C63 AMG is essentially just that, a nuclear missile with wheels. Be careful where you point it!

 Power: *457bhp*

 0-60mph: *5.2 seconds*

 Top Speed: *155mph*

 Price: *£50,000*

 Cool rating:

Mercedes C63
AMG

44

S•CK 6341

44

It doesn't always take a big engine and an even bigger price tag to make a great car. In fact, Renault keep coming up with some of the best sports cars in the world with only cheap little hatchbacks to choose from.

The secret is to make them lighter, so they're faster, and then make them handle like go-karts. The Megane R26R only gets 227bhp from its tiny 2.0-litre engine, but it's so light

and agile that it can keep up with things that have twice the power.

The real beauty of this is that making cars light and simple doesn't make them more expensive. So the R26R is the same price as your average, and very boring, Ford Mondeo.

 Power: 227bhp

 0-60mph: 6.0 seconds

 Top Speed: 147mph

 Price: £23,000

 Cool rating: 🌑🌑🌑

HK56 EFT

45

Renault Megane
R26R

'The fastest front-wheel drive car round the Nürburgring.'

46

Maserati
MC12

How does Maserati go about building a car to beat the Ferrari Enzo? Simple. It buys a Ferrari Enzo, paints it white and sticks Maserati badges on it. Then sells it to people like Jay Kay, who've already got an Enzo.

Now Ferrari actually owned Maserati at the time when the MC12 and Enzo were being made, so really this was just a cunning way of making people buy the same car twice. And considering either cost well over £400,000,

you'd want to know that the MC12 was worth it. But as it happens it probably wasn't. For starters it was slower, and to make matters worse you couldn't get over speed bumps or see out of the back.

 Power: *620bhp*

 0-60mph: *3.8 seconds*

 Top Speed: *205mph*

 Price: *£520,000*

 Cool rating:

46

In a shed somewhere in Somerset, a small group of men keep welding bits of bent scaffolding together and attaching engines. What pops out each time they do this is one of the fastest and certainly the maddest cars that *Top Gear* has ever driven.

The Ariel Atom is the car that almost sucked Jeremy's face clean off when he took it round the *Top Gear* track. And for a long time it was also at the top of our leader board, despite being powered by a 2.0-litre engine from a Honda hatchback and only costing £30,000. Bonkers then, but brilliant.

 Power: *300bhp*

 0-60mph: *2.7 seconds*

 Top Speed: *155mph*

 Price: *£30,000*

 Cool rating:

Ariel Atom
Supercharged

47

99

In the old days it was essential when designing a proper Italian supercar to make it extremely noisy, uncomfortable, almost impossible to get into, or out of, and then paint it a sickening colour.

But at some point about ten years ago everybody realised this wasn't the best way of selling lots of cars. Everyone, that is, except Lamborghini.

The LP670 is a brash, expensive and almost completely pointless car which, for all of those reasons and more besides, we absolutely love. It is huge for starters, yet tiny inside, and its 661bhp V12 makes the sort of racket that gives horses heart attacks. It also has scissor doors, and those you can't live without. Or live with, come to that.

 Power: *661bhp*

 0-60mph: *3.2 seconds*

 Top Speed: *212mph*

 Price: *£266,000*

 Cool rating:

Lamborghini
LP670-4SV

I DV·556HA BO

48

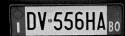

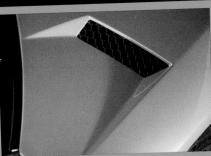

'The fastest
Lamborghini
ever made.'

49

The Ford GT was so wide, so thirsty, so fast and so flash that one of the first people in the world to buy it was a certain Jeremy Clarkson. Who would have guessed?

But there were a few hitches along the way. It took absolutely ages to arrive. And the price kept creeping up while he waited. And when it finally did get to Casa Del Clarkson the alarm kept going off in the middle of the night. It also drank so much fuel that it couldn't get him to work in the mornings on a single tank.

But it did have a 5.3-litre twin supercharged V8 that could hit 100mph in 7.4 seconds and keep going until the needle said 205. So Jeremy was happy.

 Power: 550bhp

 0-60mph: 3.5 seconds

 Top Speed: 205mph

 Price: £121,000

Cool rating:

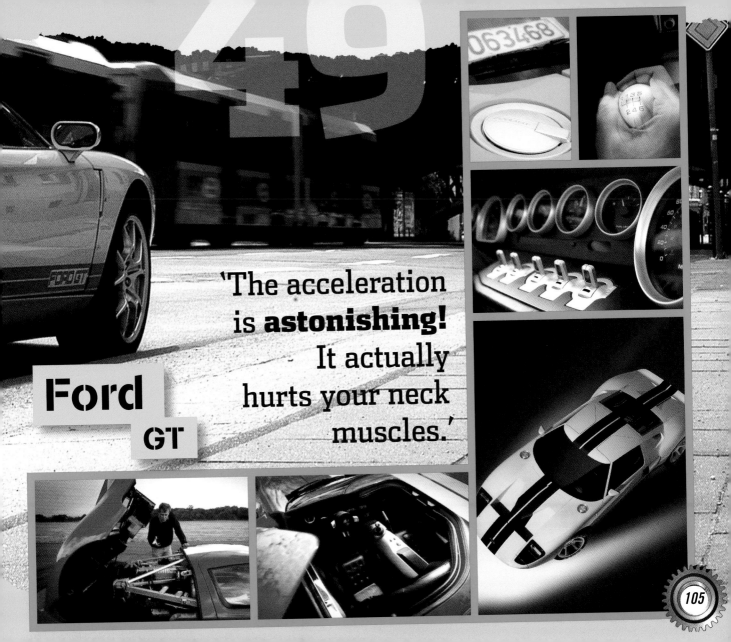

49

'The acceleration is **astonishing!** It actually hurts your neck muscles.'

Ford GT

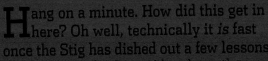

Hang on a minute. How did this get in here? Oh well, technically it *is* fast once the Stig has dished out a few lessons.

The Chevrolet Lacetti has been the (only) choice for our Star in a Reasonably-Priced Car for years now and it's still going strong. The fastest one they sell only has 119bhp, takes ten seconds to get to 60mph and is lucky if it ever gets over 100mph, but we've learnt to love it.

And remember that you can get your hands on one for just over £13,000, which is a bargain for the car that has lapped the *Top Gear* track more than any other.

Power: *119bhp*

0-60mph: *9.8 seconds*

Top Speed: *121mph*

Price: *£13,500*

Cool rating: *0*

Chevrolet
Lacetti

50

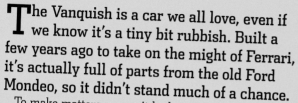

The Vanquish is a car we all love, even if we know it's a tiny bit rubbish. Built a few years ago to take on the might of Ferrari, it's actually full of parts from the old Ford Mondeo, so it didn't stand much of a chance.

To make matters worse, it had one of the first and most hopeless flappy-paddle gearboxes. This exploded at least four or five times a day, leaving premiership footballers crying on the hard shoulder all over the country.

None of this mattered a jot though, because the Vanquish didn't really need to go anywhere. Even today we reckon this is one of the best-looking supercars ever.

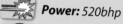

Power: *520bhp*

0-60mph: *4.8 seconds*

Top Speed: *200mph*

Price: *£177,000*

Cool rating:

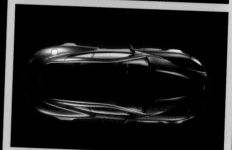

51

Aston Martin
Vanquish S

Honda Civic
Type-R

Hot hatches usually look pretty dull. Essentially just really dull cars, but with slightly bigger wheels and jazzy paint. Now the Honda Civic Type-R had a head start in this department, because the normal Civic already looked like it had come from another planet.

Give it the Type-R treatment and it still looks like it came from another planet, but at warp speed.

It gets the outer space theme on the inside too, with millions of luminous dials and switches, most of which you're too afraid to touch.

It's not actually as fast as those bonkers looks suggest, which means Jeremy absolutely hates it, but real-world speed doesn't matter when you're doing warp speed in your head.

 Power: *198bhp*

 0-60mph: *7.4 seconds*

 Top Speed: *140mph*

 Price: *£19,000*

 Cool rating:

53

Jeremy hates to admit that going fast isn't always about power, but the fifth fastest car round the *Top Gear* track definitely proves the point. The Caterham Superlight R500 has about as much oomph as your average hot hatch, but it only weighs 506kg. This adds up to 0-60mph in 2.88 seconds and a top speed of 150mph, and that's a lot in a car without a roof or doors, especially when the windscreen is an optional extra.

The most powerful car in the world, the Bugatti Veyron, took almost half a second longer to get round our track than the Caterham, and you can only buy one of them for the same price as twenty-five R500s. Which would be useless, but that's still a lot of cars.

 Power: *263bhp*

 0-60mph: *2.8 seconds*

 Top Speed: *150mph*

 Price: *£42,200*

 Cool rating: 🏁🏁🏁🏁

'It moves with the agility of a flea.'

Caterham
Superlight R500

52

The Scuderia is the Ferrari F430's leaner, meaner, younger brother. Put on a strict diet, made even more powerful and with a bucketload of computer wizardry thrown in, the Scud brought Formula 1 technology to the high street when it appeared in 2007.

Amazingly, it was as fast as the Enzo round various test tracks, but far easier for your average Joe to drive. And, at less than half the price, it was also more affordable. Well, sort of. £170,000 is still quite a lot of money.

All Scuderias also come with racing stripes running the whole length of the car, which we have to pretend to disapprove of, but secretly want to stroke when no one's looking.

 Power: 510bhp

 0-60mph: 3.6 seconds

 Top Speed: 198mph

 Price: £171,000

 Cool rating:

Ferrari F430
Scuderia

SCUDERIA
07
MO

54

The Golf GTI is widely regarded as the best all-rounder in the world. Meaning it's just as happy taking your mum to the shops as it is the Stig round our track. But now VW has thrown a spanner in the works by unveiling something it's calling the Golf R.

This is a much more powerful version of the GTI, but this time it also has four-wheel drive, which means better grip in the corners too. Which means you can go faster. Which means we now want a Volkswagen more than we want a Ford Focus RS. Oh dear. That wasn't meant to happen.

 Power: 267bhp

 0-60mph: 5.7 seconds

 Top Speed: 155mph

 Price: £30,000

 Cool rating:

55

VW Golf
R

These days most people don't even know what a Lancia is, but back in the seventies the name Stratos was on everybody's lips.

This was a car that was built with the sole purpose of winning the World Rally Championship, and it did just that for three years in a row.

With an amazing wrap-around windscreen that gave the driver the best possible view ahead, and an engine borrowed from Ferrari nestled behind the seats, this was the ultimate rally car.

But with absolutely no way of seeing behind you, and the strong likelihood that any engine borrowed from Ferrari was going to break, it wasn't quite as much fun to drive on the road.

Power: *187bhp*

0-60mph: *6.0 seconds*

Top Speed: *143mph*

Price: *£7,000 (1973)*

Cool rating:

56

Lancia
Stratos

Here's a car that is so unbelievably clever and so unbelievably fast that even people who love cars get a bit cross. Mostly because they feel like they are being left out, which is true.

The BMW M5 is really just an enormous computer with a steering wheel. And a V10 engine. It has a switch inside to limit the power for when you don't want to scare yourself silly, and all sorts of other high-tech wizardry that enables you to go supersonic without ever really noticing.

Big, posh saloons aren't meant to go supercar fast, and when they do it's all a bit too weird.

 Power: 500bhp

 0-60mph: 4.7 seconds

 Top Speed: 155mph

Price: £65,000

Cool rating: 🌡️🌡️🌡️

57

BMW M5

Nissan
GT-R

58

There was a lot of hoo-ha about the GT-R when it first came out because Nissan, who are meant to build boring cars for boring people in beige cardigans, said it was going to be better in every way than a Porsche 911 Turbo, but cost half as much.

That might have been ambitious, but the GT-R is still one of the most exciting and capable cars on sale today.

What you get is a frankly mind-boggling frenzy of technology that no one really understands, probably not even Nissan. But whatever's going on under there, it will turn your granny into a driving god. Nissan, we salute you.

Power: 478bhp

0-60mph: 3.5 seconds

Top Speed: 193mph

Price: £60,000

Cool rating: 👽👽👽

'No one has **ever** made a car like this before.'

59

Corvette
Z06

It's generally accepted that America makes rubbish cars. Even Americans will tell you this. But every now and again they do something rather special, and the Corvette Z06 is just one of those somethings.

Using ideas from their Le Mans-winning racing cars, the Z06 is not only blisteringly fast, but also capable of doing something that's almost unheard of in the US. It can go round corners.

There's also a truly massive 7.0-litre V8 gurgling under that bonnet, pushing out 512bhp and enormous dollops of torque. And on top of that, it's half the price of most Italian or German supercars. Bargain.

 Power: *512bhp*

0-60mph: *3.9 seconds*

Top Speed: *198mph*

Price: *£65,000*

 Cool rating:

59

60

Audi R8
V10

'This car is almost without fault.
It is absolutely **stunning**.'

124

A few years ago Audi only made cars for dads. And pretty boring dads at that. They were all just a bit too sensible. Then something weird happened. Something that made the bosses at places like Ferrari go grey overnight. Audi made a supercar.

The R8 manages to do everything that normal, boring Audis do, like being easy to drive, and really reliable and comfortable, while also being able to do things that Ferraris can do, like go round corners faster than a jet fighter and make girls faint at 1000 yards.

Amazing to look at, simple to live with and terrifyingly fast – this really might be *the* best car in the world today. But we say that about everything.

 Power: 518bhp

 0-60mph: 3.9 seconds

 Top Speed: 196mph

 Price: £99,500

 Cool rating:

Not wanting to be left out of the supercar showdown, Mercedes asked its F1 chums at McLaren to build something to put the wind up Ferrari, Porsche and the rest. They came up with the SLR, essentially a gigantic bonnet with some wheels stuck on at the last minute.

With its 617bhp supercharged 6.0-litre V8, the SLR ticks all sorts of supercar boxes. It'll comfortably pass 200mph for instance, and hit 60mph in a little over three seconds.

What McLaren forgot, however, was to make this £347,000 hypercar any fun to drive. So Mercedes has stopped building it.

  Power: *617bhp*

 0-60mph: *3.8 seconds*

 Top Speed: *208mph*

 Price: *£347,000*

 Cool rating:

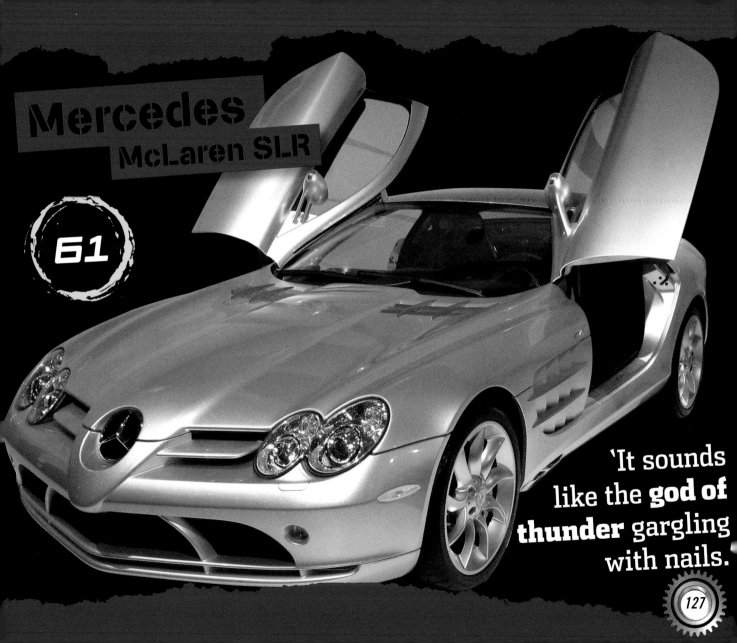

Mercedes
McLaren SLR

61

'It sounds like the **god of thunder** gargling with nails.

Ferrari
P4/5

If owning a Ferrari Enzo sounds a bit boring, your name must be James Glickenhaus. For James, who we can only guess has quite a bit of money stashed under his mattress, decided to spend around £3 million getting Ferrari to build him his very own car, based on an Enzo, but with even cooler styling.

The P4/5 uses the same chassis as the Enzo but with an all-new body that combines the classic looks of various sixties racing Ferraris with the latest advances in modern aerodynamics.

What this adds up to is a car that is not only way more beautiful than an Enzo, but also faster and more stable at high speed. Perhaps Mr Glickenhaus isn't as mad as we thought...

Power: 660bhp

0-60mph: 3.5 seconds

Top Speed: 225mph

Price: £3million

Cool rating:

62

612 P4-5
NEW YORK
THE EMPIRE STATE

129

'Aaaaaarrggghh!!'

Porsche 911 GT2

63

While the likes of Ferrari and Lamborghini get their knickers in a twist about building exotic cars in strange shades of yellow, Porsche just gets on with the business of winning races. And the 911 GT2 is about as close as you can get to owning a proper racing Porsche that'll still take you to the supermarket on a Sunday morning.

This car has an engine half the size of a Ferrari Enzo, but it's almost as powerful and only half a second slower round the *Top Gear* track. And you could have three of them for the price of an Enzo, or just the one and a large house. (We'd get three.)

Power: *530bhp*

0-60mph: *3.7 seconds*

Top Speed: *204mph*

Price: *£131,000*

Cool rating: 😀😀😀😀

63

Ascari
A10

Just like the Gumpert Apollo that pipped it for top spot on the *Top Gear* track, the Ascari A10 is really a racing car. This means that you don't get creature-comforts like air conditioning, or even a stereo, and instead you have a roll cage, which is essentially like giving a lift to some scaffolding.

The upside of all this is that the 635bhp Ascari A10 will hit 60mph in just 2.8 seconds and won't run out of puff until 220mph. The downside is that it'll set you back £350,000, or two Ferrari 458s and some change, which is a whole lot of pocket money. You decide.

 Power: 635bhp

 0-60mph: 2.8 seconds

 Top Speed: 220mph

 Price: £350,000

 Cool rating:

64

'It's **quicker** than almost anything.'

OU55 GWJ

A Sagaris is an ancient Greek battleaxe. Naming cars after old weapons is a very good idea, especially if they are potentially a bit lethal, which the TVR Sagaris definitely is.

Almost all cars these days have things like airbags and traction control to stop people getting hurt. But not the Sagaris. Or any TVR for that matter. This is a car that depends entirely on the skill of its driver, but one that will still hit 60mph in under four seconds and keep on going to 185mph.

Although we love the Sagaris, we probably wouldn't want to own one. Or be anywhere near one that was moving.

 Power: *406bhp*

 0-60mph: *3.8 seconds*

 Top Speed: *185mph*

 Price: *£50,000*

 Cool rating:

TVR

Sagaris

65

66

'This is a **brilliant** car. It does everything **brilliantly**.'

BMW
M3

The difference between a normal BMW and one with an 'M' stuck on its bum is basically like the difference between the smallest kid in school and the headmaster. One has all the power and he likes to dish out the occasional punishment.

The BMW M3 takes a very common and fairly dull German saloon, chucks out the rear doors, squeezes an enormous V8 under the bonnet and turns double-glazing salesmen into racing drivers.

This probably makes double-glazing salesmen even more unpopular than they already are, but at least they're happy now. And wherever it is they're going, they're definitely getting there faster than us.

 Power: *414bhp*

 0-60mph: *4.8 seconds*

 Top Speed: *155mph*

 Price: *£51,000*

 Cool rating: 🏁🏁🏁🏁

66

Lamborghini
Gallardo Spyder

DS·699FR

67

140

Strictly speaking, *Top Gear* doesn't approve of soft top versions of proper supercars. Cutting the roof off something usually makes it heavier and, well, a bit girly. But we have to make an exception for the Gallardo Spyder. Here is a car that looks more beautiful as a soft top, which is a seriously difficult thing to do, and doesn't give up anything in terms of proper supercar-ness in the process.

Although a smidgen slower than the coupé through the gears, the latest version, called the LP-560-4, will still pass 200mph. That was good enough for Jeremy, because he actually went and bought one. (Which might explain where all his hair is going.)

Power: *552bhp*

0-60mph: *4.0 seconds*

Top Speed: *201mph*

Price: *£152,000*

Cool rating:

141

68

Renault Clio
Cup

142

Not everything that's fast has to be big, powerful and expensive. In fact one of the fastest cars on sale today is tiny, not at all powerful and cheap as chips. And even more strangely, it's made by Renault.

The little Clio Cup is a firm favourite at *Top Gear*. You could buy around eighty of them for the price of one Bugatti Veyron, and on most days, on most roads, the Clio would be the faster car.

This is because it's like a roller skate with an engine. Brilliant at zipping around towns and through winding country roads where the Veyron would probably just get stuck, the Cup might just be the perfect car for busy little Britain. Don't buy eighty though. That would be stupid.

Power: *197bhp*

0-60mph: *6.9 seconds*

Top Speed: *141mph*

Price: *£16,000*

Cool rating:

59

Lotus Exige
S

69

Tucked away in a corner of Norfolk, surrounded by fields, mud and not much else, a small group of blokes tinker away day and night, making some of the best cars in the world.

The thing about the Lotus Exige is that, although not the fastest car in a straight line, as soon as you have to go round a corner there's nothing in our solar system to touch it. And there are a lot of corners in our solar system.

Add that to the fact that it looks like an alien attack fighter and is usually painted in the sort of colour you wouldn't even trust in an ice cream, and you have the recipe for success – *Top Gear* style.

Power: *218bhp*

0-60mph: *4.5 seconds*

Top Speed: *148mph*

Price: *£34,000*

Cool rating: 😀😀😀😀

The eighties wasn't a great time for Ferrari. They'd made some pretty shoddy cars for the road and weren't doing that well on the racetrack either. So a decision was made to sort out both problems at once. Enter the F40.

This was a Ferrari like no other. It was so focused on lightweight performance that even things like door handles were dispensed with in favour of a bit of string you had to pull. There were no carpets either, and all the glass wasn't actually glass, it was plastic.

This didn't stop the F40 costing a small fortune however. But nor did it stop it being the fastest production car of its time, and the first to pass 200mph.

 Power: *478bhp*

 0-60mph: *3.9 seconds*

 Top Speed: *201mph*

 **Price:** *£193,000*

Cool rating:

Ferrari
F40

70

70

146

Back in the sixties Ford tried to buy Ferrari, but at the last minute Ferrari decided it wasn't for sale. This made Ford rather angry, so to teach them a lesson it built a car designed solely to thrash Ferrari in every race it could.

The GT40 is so called because it is only 40-inches high. This means you have to be Richard Hammond to drive it, but it also means it handles brilliantly. Which was great news for Ford and bad news for Ferrari.

For four years running, the GT40 won the Le Mans 24 Hours, the toughest motor race in the world, demolishing Ferrari and anyone else who dared turn up. Job done.

Power: 350bhp

0-60mph: 4.6 seconds

Top Speed: 187mph

Price: £6,000 (1966)

Cool rating:

71 **Ford**
GT40

It won't have escaped your attention that supercars aren't the most practical things in the world. Almost no storage space and only two doors mean they're not exactly the ideal family car. In fact they're basically useless unless you have a very small girlfriend and only own one pair of pants.

But there is change afoot. Following hot on the heels of the unspeakably ugly and boring Porsche Panamera is the Aston Martin Rapide.

Perhaps James Bond dropped a hint that he was about to settle down, get married and have children, but whatever the reason, Aston has created the perfect blend of sensational sportscar and sensible saloon.

A 188mph V12 supercar with room in the back for a couple of young petrolheads? Tell Dad to start saving...

Power: *470bhp*

0-60mph: *5.1 seconds*

Top Speed: *188mph*

Price: *£140,000*

Cool rating:

72

Aston Martin
Rapide

149

When British people get bored they start growing their own veg or painting watercolours. In Germany they make things like the Brabus Biturbo. This is a Mercedes SL which some men with far too much time on their hands turned into the most powerful convertible ever. At the time anyway.

Despite having a name that sounds like an embarrassing case of wind, the Brabus is not a car for the faint-hearted. Those bored men who made it actually had to put an electronic limit on the car's ridiculous top speed. But being German, the limit they settled on was 219mph. Good boys.

 Power: 730bhp

 0-60mph: 4.0 seconds

 Top Speed: 219mph

 Price: £160,000

 Cool rating: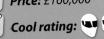

Brabus Biturbo
Roadster

Pick-up trucks are big business in Australia, birthplace of the Holden Maloo. But this is no ordinary pick-up, even by their standards.

Despite having more space for sheep than people, you get a Corvette's 6.0-litre V8 wedged under that bonnet, sending 410bhp to the rear wheels. This means the Maloo can cover the quarter mile in 13.8 seconds. And farmers simply aren't meant to do that.

The Maloo is really just a pick-up version of the Monaro, that beefcake Vauxhall coupé that Jeremy drove like a hooligan until his back gave out. Except that this thing doesn't even pretend to have a practical daily purpose, unless that purpose is scaring sheep to death.

 Power: 410bhp

 0-60mph: 5.0 seconds

 Top Speed: 160mph

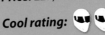 **Price:** £27,000

 Cool rating: 😊😊😊

Holden
Maloo

74

74

'This is the **fastest** ute in the world.'

OU58 FMD

DE51 RED

75

Tesla Roadster

154

75

What you've got here is a window into the future. A crystal ball, if you like. And it's sort of Lotus-shaped.

This is the Tesla Roadster, an all-electric sports car based loosely on the Lotus Elise. This means it's small and pretty basic, but handles like a proper sports car should. What's different, of course, is that there isn't an engine anywhere to be seen. Or a gearbox. Instead you just get an eerily quiet electric motor that hurtles you about, without so much as a whisper.

There is a problem though. Tesla claims the car will do around 200 miles on a single charge. Drive it fast (it is a sports car, after all) and you'd be lucky to manage half that. Oops.

 Power: *288bhp*

 0-60mph: *3.9 seconds*

 Top Speed: *130mph*

 Price: *£90,000*

 Cool rating: 🎭🎭

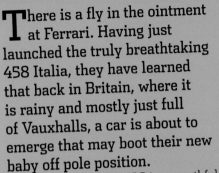**T**here is a fly in the ointment at Ferrari. Having just launched the truly breathtaking 458 Italia, they have learned that back in Britain, where it is rainy and mostly just full of Vauxhalls, a car is about to emerge that may boot their new baby off pole position.

The McLaren MP4-12C is a mouthful to say, but it's one you should probably practise. Here is the successor to the McLaren F1, a supercar still regarded by most people as the greatest ever, despite being twenty years old.

The MP4-12C will use technology from McLaren's Formula 1 racing cars and the latest ideas from scientific boffins to be incredibly fast but also economical and nice to the environment. Look out Ferrari, the British are coming...

 Power: 600bhp

 0-60mph: 3.0 seconds (approx)

 Top Speed: 200+mph

 Price: £160,000 (approx)

 Cool rating:

McLaren
MP4-12C

'76

MP4-12C

Jaguar
XKR

Now, Jags tend to be the choice of granddads with fake tans and nowhere to go in a hurry. The XKR, though, is a very different creature. This is the car that stuck it to Porsche and Aston Martin in one fell swoop by being beautiful, fast and amazingly comfortable.

The XKR manages to match the gracefulness of an Aston for the price of a Porsche. And it still has a 503bhp V8 to play with. But the most amazing thing about Jaguar's super-coupé is how it can drive like a sports car and still feel like a limousine. Going anywhere in this car is like taking your private jet. Granddads will love it, but so will you.

 Power: 503bhp

 0-60mph: 4.6 seconds

 Top Speed: 155mph

 Price: £72,000

 Cool rating: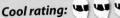

77

78

If you grow up to be a really rich playboy type, probably living on the French Riviera in a huge house with a glamorous wife, you'd be expected to drive a Ferrari. Or a Lamborghini if you were daring.

So the only way to stand out from the Ferrari and/or Lamborghini-driving crowd is to get the Fiat 500 Abarth.

It's Italian, which is good. Most playboys insist on that. It's also a tiny hatchback, and they're great for zipping around town. (Playboys only leave town in private jets.) And it's ridiculously fast for something so small, so you can embarrass the supercar big boys and still find somewhere to park. Which is vital, as playboys spend the whole time shopping.

Power: *133bhp*

0-60mph: *7.9 seconds*

Top Speed: *128mph*

Price: *£13,500*

Cool rating:

Fiat 500 Abarth

163

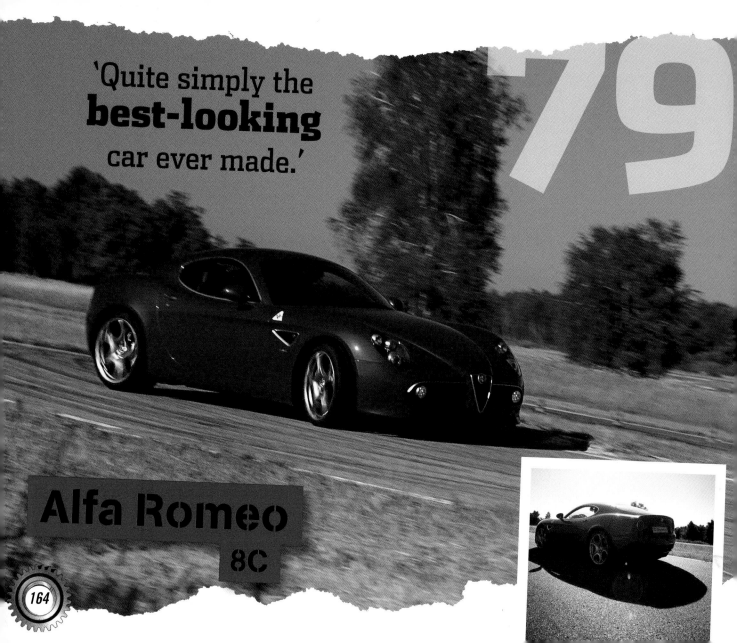

'Quite simply the **best-looking** car ever made.'

Alfa Romeo

8C

There's this really annoying thing that car companies do sometimes to make people pay them more attention. They design an absolutely amazing car, then announce that they're only going to make a handful of them. And that every single one of them has already been sold.

This is what happened with Alfa Romeo's beautiful 8C. No one could quite believe that Alfa could make such a fabulous thing, a sort of cross between a supercar and a supermodel.

Devastatingly fast and utterly gorgeous, we all wanted to see it go up against the likes of Aston Martin and Ferrari. But all the 8Cs have disappeared into private garages, never to be seen again.

 Power: *450bhp*

 0-60mph: *4.5 seconds*

 Top Speed: *190mph*

 Price: *£100,000*

 Cool rating: 😎😎😎😎😎

79

Bowler
Wildcat

Land Rover is famous for making one of the best off-roaders in the world. It'll go anywhere, do anything and take a lot of punishment in the process. But everything has to be done very, very slowly.

That's where Bowler come in. They took the good bits off a Land Rover and turned it into an off-road race car, with lighter body panels, competition suspension and 5.0-litre V8 race-tuned engines.

The Wildcat competes in the toughest races the world can throw at it, driving up the sides of mountains and across thousands of miles of desert. And it can still do the school run when you get it home again.

 Power: 265bhp

 0-60mph: 4.8 seconds

 Top Speed: 115mph

 Price: £50,000

 Cool rating:

'I am a driving god!'

80

167

There's something mischievous going on at Mercedes these days. All those boring silver cars driven by old people wearing toupees and grey shoes have gone and got a bit, well, black.

The SL Black is a 670bhp, 6.0-litre twin-turbo V12 monster with gigantic flared wheel arches and a fixed carbon fibre roof. It's lighter and harder than your average SL, and it's also a serious handful.

Turning ordinary SLs into beefed-up supercars is all very well, but the upshot is what Jeremy called 'the most uncomfortable car in all of human history'. Which might just put you off spending a lifetime's worth of pocket money.

 Power: 670bhp

 0-60mph: 3.7 seconds

 Top Speed: 199mph

 Price: £265,000

 Cool rating:

Mercedes SL
Black

KX58 KWZ

81

Audi makes lots of ordinary cars for ordinary people. But it also has dibs on something we call 'Q cars'. These always look pretty normal. A standard saloon, for example, with four doors, a boot and someone like your dad behind the wheel. But they hide a dark and awesome secret...

The beefy wheel arches and fat twin exhaust pipes of the RS4 are your first clues that there is something very special going on under that bonnet, namely a 414bhp 4.2-litre V8 engine. As you might expect, this is one of the fastest saloons the world has ever seen. And it also has special racing seats that tighten around the driver when he goes round a corner, which is too cool for words.

 Power: 414bhp

 0-60mph: 4.9 seconds

 Top Speed: 155mph

 Price: £50,000

 Cool rating:

Audi
RS4

82

HN·QU 312

RS4

171

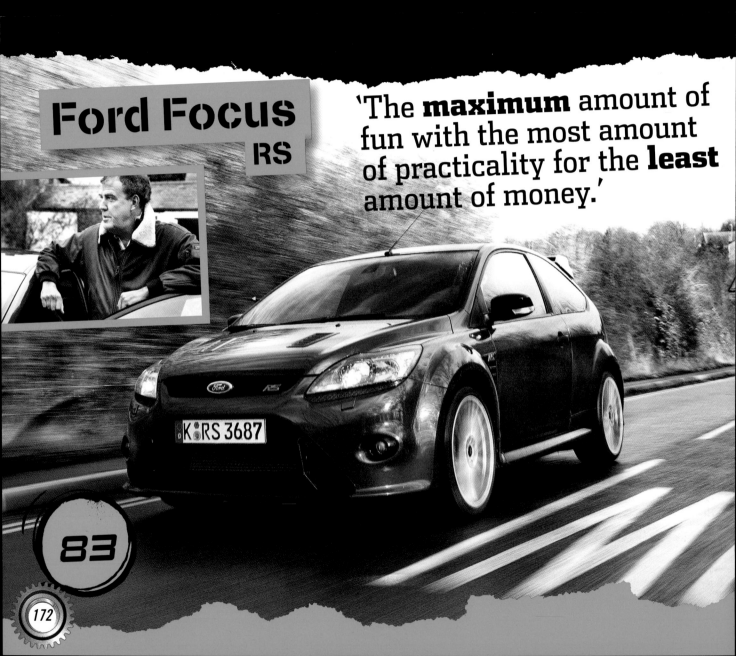

Ford Focus RS

'The **maximum** amount of fun with the most amount of practicality for the **least** amount of money.'

83

172

This is what happens when the spirit of an American muscle car gets crammed into a small, British hatchback. The Focus RS is a shouty brute of a thing, with its turbocharged engine, flared wheel arches and body-coloured bucket seats.

But there's another side to the RS. This thing may have the looks and attitude of the school bully, but it behaves like the teacher's pet when it's out on the open road. And this is exactly what makes a great car: all the power and presence of the scariest of sports cars, but with the manners of your mum's runabout. Top of the class.

 Power: *301bhp*

 0-60mph: *5.9 seconds*

 Top Speed: *164mph*

 Price: *£26,000*

 Cool rating:

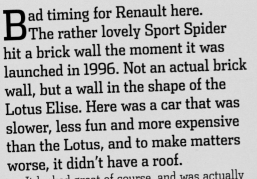

Bad timing for Renault here. The rather lovely Sport Spider hit a brick wall the moment it was launched in 1996. Not an actual brick wall, but a wall in the shape of the Lotus Elise. Here was a car that was slower, less fun and more expensive than the Lotus, and to make matters worse, it didn't have a roof.

It looked great of course, and was actually quite good to drive, but none of that really mattered when you couldn't drive it anywhere in case it rained. And you had to spend the whole time explaining to people why you didn't just buy an Elise.

Renault gave up making the Spider after only a year and a half. Oh dear.

Power: 144bhp

0-60mph: 6.5 seconds

Top Speed: 131mph

Price: £25,000

Cool rating: 😎😎

Renault Sport
Spider

84

Lancia Delta
Integrale

85

Although Lancia has never made a car that anyone expects to work for more than about five minutes, it doesn't stop us loving them. Well, the fast ones at any rate. And there were few faster than the Delta Integrale.

This was a car that Lancia used in the World Rally Championship back in the 1980s, and the road-going version quickly became a bit of a legend. It looked brilliant, with all those angles and edges and flared wheel arches, and it was genuinely quick with its turbocharged engine and grippy four-wheel drive.

The only problem was that Lancia never made them in right-hand drive, which means if you wanted one in Britain, you had to drive it from the passenger seat.

Power: 200bhp

0-60mph: 6.3 seconds

Top Speed: 129mph

Price: £25,000 (1993)

Cool rating:

BMW Z4M

The Z4M is one of those cars that reminds even the bravest of drivers that there are limits, and that if you want to get home for tea, limits need to be respected.

These aren't speed limits we're talking about either (although they are rather important), but the limits of physics. BMW has made a tiny, fidgety car that dishes out the power like confetti at a wedding, but can't quite put it on the road.

This is the sort of car that *Top Gear* absolutely loves, just so long as it's not snowing. Or raining. Or a bit dark. And only if the Stig is driving.

Power: 330bhp

0-60mph: 4.8 seconds

Top Speed: 155mph

Price: £43,000

Cool rating: 🏎🏎🏎🏎🏎

86

87

GY08 HNU

L exus is Toyota's posh brand. The idea is that it can make loads more money by putting a different badge on the front of really boring Japanese saloons. And it works a treat.

The IS-F is a bit different though. It's not trying to be posh. It's trying to beat the BMW M3 into a pulp. And it does.

Looking fairly ordinary as it trundles silently about its business, the IS-F hides a naughty little secret beneath that bulging bonnet. Attached to a race-speed flappy-paddle gearbox is an incredible 417bhp 5.0-litre V8. This can whisk the IS-F to almost 170mph, leaving the M3 sobbing in the weeds.

 Power: *417bhp*

 0-60mph: *5.2 seconds*

 Top Speed: *168mph*

 Price: *£55,000*

 Cool rating:

Lexus
IS-F

One of the grand traditions of the sports car is to fit it with two completely useless rear seats. The sort of thing that not even your little brother would be comfortable in, even if you could fit the now-essential booster seat. Which you almost never can.

Maybe the boss of Maserati has a couple of young 'uns then, because his latest two-door coupé, the GranTurismo, has proper back seats, the likes of which are good enough for tiny babies and even the lanky teenagers they become.

There's still 433bhp to play with though, which means you can hit 183mph. And that's pretty fast for a crèche on wheels.

 Power: 433bhp

 0-60mph: 4.9 seconds

 Top Speed: 183mph

Price: £88,000

 **Cool rating:**

88

Maserati
Gran Turismo S

KTM
X-Bow

GD20PA

Bored of making some of the best motorbikes in the world, Austrian outfit KTM decided to build a car. But years of making bikes had evidently confused KTM as to what cars actually looked like, so instead they came up with a bath made out of carbon fibre.

This wasn't necessarily such a bad idea though, since this bath did have wheels, and bolted to the back, where you might have expected to find the shower attachment, was a turbocharged engine from Audi.

What's more, this bath/wheels/engine idea only weighed 700kg and, with the engine easily tuned to over 300bhp, it went fast enough to push your ears to the back of your head. Good job there were lots of motorbike helmets lying around.

Power: *300bhp*

0-60mph: *3.5 seconds*

Top Speed: *140mph*

Price: *£60,000*

Cool rating:

89

183

90

'It is **fantastic.**'

Aston Martin
V12 Vantage

184

KX09 GXP

90

When the new V8 Vantage appeared everybody loved the looks, but wished it had a bit more power. Aston realised they had the DBS sitting around while James Bond was off duty, so they pinched the 6.0-litre V12 engine out of that and somehow managed to wedge it into the Vantage.

The result was a car that left Jeremy almost lost for words, and that takes some doing. All he could manage was 'wonderful, wonderful, wonderful.' Suddenly there was more than enough power, more menacing looks and, at long last, a car that even Clarkson couldn't criticise.

 Power: 510bhp

 0-60mph: 4.1 seconds

 Top Speed: 190mph

 Price: £135,000

 Cool rating:

185

'It presses all the right **supercar** buttons.'

91

188

Lotus Evora

If you want to make money these days you have to be ready to take on the big boys. That means little companies like Lotus need to come up with something as good as the latest Porsche or BMW. And that's never going to be very easy.

The Elise was a bit too rough 'n' ready, so Lotus designed a car with more space, more creature comforts, more power and more, well, posh. Meet the Evora, a £50,000 sports car to steal customers from things like the Porsche Cayman.

It's still made of plastic though, just like an Elise, and its 3.0-litre V6 comes out of a rubbish old Toyota. Despite all that, it's really rather good, but can a Lotus ever be better than a Porsche? We're undecided.

 Power: 276bhp

 0-60mph: 4.9 seconds

 Top Speed: 162mph

 Price: £47,500

 Cool rating: 🏁🏁🏁🏁

Morgan
Aeromax

Morgan makes cars out of wood. This is not quite as daft as it seems because wood is cheap, easy to use and surprisingly good in a crash. But it's still, let's face it, pretty daft.

Which might explain why our own Richard Hammond thought it would be a fine idea to buy the Morgan Aeromax.

This is the sort of car you can only really imagine being bought by Batman. When he's retired and needs something to pop to the post office in on pension day. It looks more like a medieval castle than a car, and has some fairly medieval technology to go with it.

Morgan says they're only ever going to build 100 Aeromax, but considering it costs twice as much as the normal Aero 8 roadster, that's already quite brave.

 Power: 362bhp

 0-60mph: 4.2 seconds

 Top Speed: 170mph

 Price: £110,000

 Cool rating:

92

92.

93

For absolutely years, Toyota's posh brand Lexus had been promising to make a supercar to scare the pants off Ferrari and Porsche. We'd all been nodding politely and smiling and had pretty much given up on ever seeing it, when suddenly the LFA appeared. Looking like a very badly-made paper dart.

But it was fast. Seriously fast. And sounded like the engine had been stolen from a Formula 1 racing car.

The only problem was it took Lexus so long to make the LFA that they decided to charge twice the price of the same sort of Ferrari or Porsche. And no one wants to spend that on a Toyota, do they?

 Power: *525bhp*

 0-60mph: *3.7 seconds*

 Top Speed: *202mph*

 Price: *£330,000*

 Cool rating: 😈 😈 😈 😈

Lexus
LFA

'That's really **quite** a fast car.'

Now it's a sad fact, but most of us won't be spending our lives pootling to the shops and back in Ferraris and Lamborghinis. Unless we all manage to get jobs with Manchester United, and that's looking doubtful. But there is hope for us yet, and it comes in the shape of the Golf GTI.

Yes, it's only a Volkswagen, and yes, it's just a hatchback with a weedy 2.0-litre engine. But strangely, the Golf GTI might just be the best car in the world.

Not only is it really useful, with its big boot and back seat, but it's also cheap, comfy and really quite smart inside. And around windy country roads instead of racetracks, there are few cars that can go faster. Three cheers for Volkswagen.

 Power: *207bhp*

 0-60mph: *6.9 seconds*

 Top Speed: *149mph*

 Price: *£23,000*

 Cool rating:

VW Golf
GTI

94

195

Ferrari 599
GTB

The frightening thing about working for Ferrari is that you build 'The Best Car in the World', and then ten minutes later the boss asks you to do it all over again.

But could the 599 GTB be as good as it gets? Stunning to look at, easy to drive, and, at 612bhp, the most powerful road car Ferrari has ever made.

Quick cars these days will get to 60mph in under eight seconds. The 599 gets to 100mph in less than that and will keep on going to well past 200mph.

So is this really the ultimate all-round supercar? For ten minutes, maybe.

 Power: 612bhp

 0-60mph: 3.7 seconds

Top Speed: 205mph

Price: £198,000

 Cool rating:

95

'This is my new **favourite** car.'

Mercedes
CLK Black

96

Some cars don't even have to be very good to be great. The Mercedes CLK Black gets an awful lot of things completely wrong, but ends up being one of the most awesome things Merc has made in years.

Styled on one of the extreme and slightly terrifying cars that compete in Germany's DTM race series, the CLK Black has the mean and muscular look of an all-out racing car with flared arches, huge rear wing, bucket seats and lightweight carbon fibre trim.

But the gearbox is rubbish, it's horrendously uncomfortable and it sounds like it's got a terrible case of wind. None of that matters of course, because the Black is all about driving drama. Not even half as good on the road as a Porsche 911 Turbo, it's still ten times more exciting.

 Power: 507bhp

 0-60mph: 4.3 seconds

 Top Speed: 186mph

 Price: £100,000

 Cool rating:

Lamborghini
Reventón

If the Batmobile had a flat tyre, this would have to be your next port of call. The Lamborghini Reventón is a slightly more powerful version of the Murcielago, but with styling that was probably borrowed from a stealth bomber.

The Reventón gets its name from a famous and particularly scary bull, which seems appropriate, and benefits from all sorts of space-age magic inside, like digital instruments instead of conventional dials.

Only twenty were ever made and Lamborghini had no trouble finding buyers, despite the fact that the Reventón cost nearly £900,000. That's doubly bonkers when you think that the normal Murcielago is a whisker over £200,000 and actually just as fast.

 Power: 641bhp

 0-60mph: 3.4 seconds

 Top Speed: 211mph

 Price: £850,000

 Cool rating: 🎭🎭🎭🎭

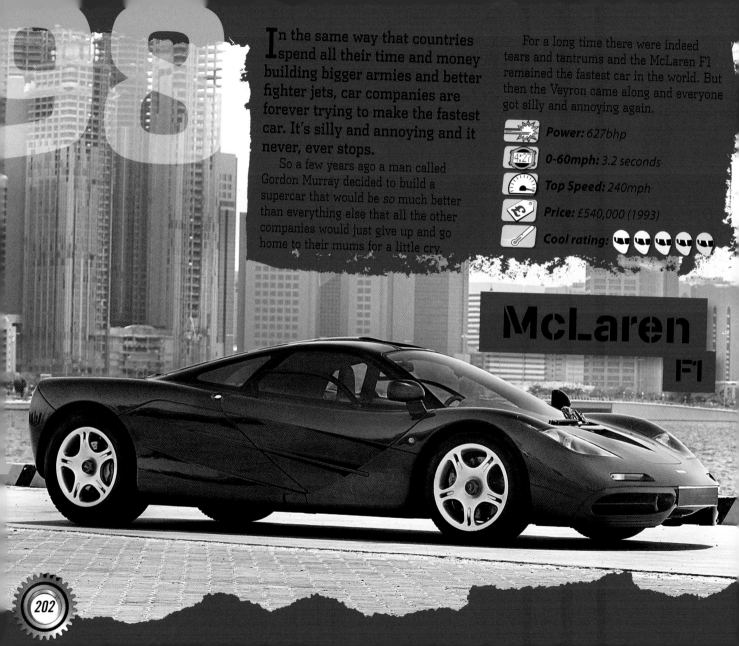

In the same way that countries spend all their time and money building bigger armies and better fighter jets, car companies are forever trying to make the fastest car. It's silly and annoying and it never, ever stops.

So a few years ago a man called Gordon Murray decided to build a supercar that would be *so* much better than everything else that all the other companies would just give up and go home to their mums for a little cry.

For a long time there were indeed tears and tantrums and the McLaren F1 remained the fastest car in the world. But then the Veyron came along and everyone got silly and annoying again.

Power: *627bhp*

0-60mph: *3.2 seconds*

Top Speed: *240mph*

Price: *£540,000 (1993)*

Cool rating:

McLaren
F1

Porsche
Cayman S

Any car that Jeremy openly hates should automatically attract your attention, because chances are it's a) a Porsche, and b) very good indeed.

The Cayman S is just such a car. So German and so utterly brilliant that if one ever turned up at Clarkson Castle it would probably be set on fire.

A mid-engined, less powerful and less expensive version of the legendary 911, the Cayman is just as good as its big brother, and when being driven at race speeds by slightly boring expert driver types, apparently it's actually even better.

Worth remembering, but just don't tell Jeremy.

Power: 316bhp

0-60mph: 5.2 seconds

Top Speed: 171mph

Price: £44,500

Cool rating:

Cayman S

100

Zenvo
ST1

100

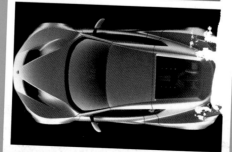

Denmark is famous for being next to Sweden. And maybe for bacon. But that's about it. Or at least it was, until the Zenvo ST1 came along. This is Denmark's first supercar, and it's one we need to pay attention to.

Not only does it look like nothing else on earth, but it sounds and goes like it too. The ST1 has 1,100bhp, which is more than the Bugatti Veyron, and all that out of an engine with half as many cylinders.

There is a catch, however. If you intend to rustle up the £800,000 required to buy a Zenvo, you're going to have to do it fast. Only 15 ST1s are ever going to be made. Don't ask us why.

Power: *1,100bhp*

0-60mph: *3.0 seconds*

Top Speed: *233mph*

Price: *£800,000*

Cool rating:

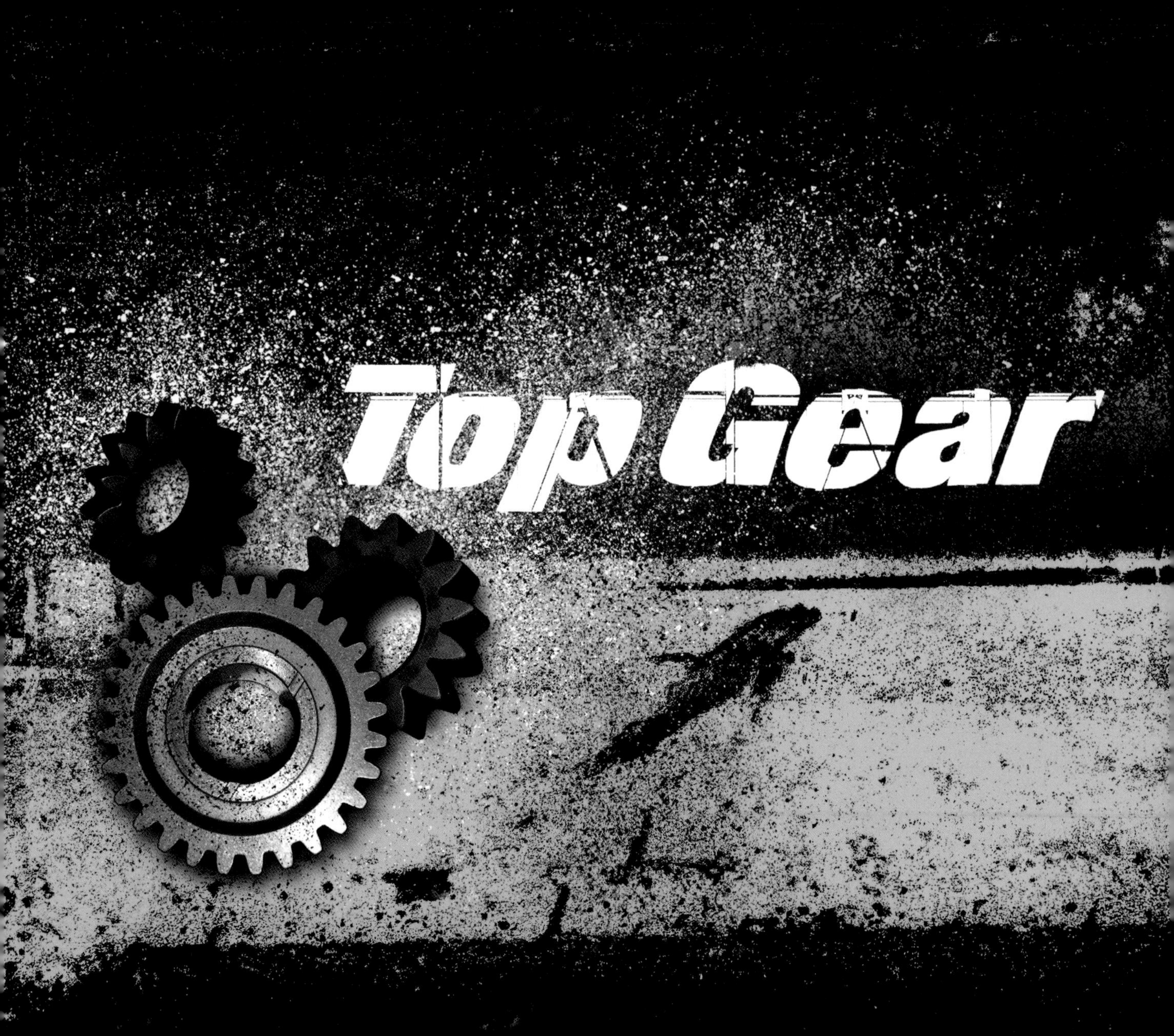
Top Gear